The Roots of My Trichotillomania

How I made peace with myself

DOUGLAS G MacKENZIE

DEDICATION

This book is dedicated to all of the beautiful people who struggle with disorders such as trichotillomania.

CONTENTS

ACKNOWLEDGMENTS

I would like to thank Carole Wicks for helping me to get here, and Malcolm Turner for suggesting some edits to the text. Finally, thanks to Nina for everything.

INTRODUCTION

This book describes a phenomenon called trichotillomania, which is best characterized as a behavioural disorder that involves people pulling out their hair compulsively. Information about the exact description of the disorder and the wide range of treatment options that are available can be found easily from internet sources. This isn't that kind of book. This book describes my own personal experience with hair pulling, how the disorder developed and what it feels like to struggle with a condition that is not yet well understood.

The first part of the book describes my early life around the time I began pulling out my hair and how I spent many years struggling to cope with and to understand the disorder. Next, I offer up my own speculations about what motivates or predisposes people to pull their hair out. This isn't hard science, but it is underpinned by years of my own research around the topic. As you will come to realise, there hasn't been very much research done, which means that clinicians and individuals who try to treat trichotillomania are in many ways scrambling about in the dark. After that, the book describes my most recent thinking about my problem with trichotillomania, summarises what I have learned and how I plan to move forward. Finally, the book closes with a question and answer session, where I answer the most obvious questions that I think people might want to ask me about trichotillomania.

DECLINE AND FALL

One day when I was sixteen years old I was revising for my school exams and I started pulling hair out from my scalp. I had been spending some time twisting hair with my fingers, wrapping individual hairs around my fingertips, and then with no forethought I yanked a hair out. It caused a strange sensation — none of the pain that you would imagine, but rather more of a slight high feeling. I looked at the hair I had pulled out and saw that there was a white, gelatinous cylinder covering the

4

root. I felt strange about pulling it out, wondered what to do with it, and then dropped it on the floor next to me. I was reading The Great Gatsby for my Higher English exam. It was the third time I had read the book, and to some extent I was reading it automatically. I could read about Jay Gatsby looking over at the light on Daisy's dock at night whilst diverting some of my attention away from the story and towards what I was doing with my fingers and hair. I found that I pulled out a second hair, and then a third and a fourth, with what seemed like no volition at all on my part. I got really scared. I told myself not to pull another hair out, but as I continued reading I noticed that my left hand went up to my scalp again, found another hair and pulled it out. The neutral feeling I had when pulling out the first few hairs was replaced by fear and anger. I berated myself. I told myself to stop, that no good could come of this. I tried sitting on my hand but that didn't work. After a while I just took my hand out from under my leg and reached for my head. I tried holding the book in my left hand but even then I found myself putting down the book and pulling out more of my hair. I was scared of what I was doing and I didn't tell anybody about it because I was freaked out and I felt ashamed.

I have continued pulling hair out from my scalp and other places on my body in this compulsive manner for over twenty years now. It has blighted my life. I have feared for my sanity at times. I have dropped out of university courses, left jobs and avoided relationships as a direct result of this strange behaviour that I cannot control. More recently, I have also come to discover that I am not alone. Through the internet I have discovered that many other people get stuck in this self-destructive routine and can neither control it nor escape from it. I became a father a few years ago and I am terrified that my children might inherit this awful disorder. I have decided to describe here and try to explain what compulsive hair pulling is like partly to understand myself better and partly to explain trichotillomania to my children and other loved ones. I hope what follows may be of some interest to anybody else who is affected by hair pulling.

Memory is a tricky thing. Some events remain clear in my mind while other things that happened around the same time seem forever lost. To make matters worse, I know that whenever we access a memory we subtly change it. I have gone over much of my past many times, and however confident I feel about some memories I understand that some things may not have happened quite how I recall them now, especially as I try to recount what happened to me in the first few years after starting to pull out my hair.

I remember fear. I remember with a cold certainty that I was scared about pulling out my hair. I was scared about what my family and friends and even strangers might say to me or even think about me but most of all I was scared about myself. I was really scared because I made a strong effort not to pull hair yet I did it all the same. No matter what I tried, whenever I was alone I would pull. I felt like my will power was divorced from control over my hand and it terrified me. I guess I was horrified by the implications this had for my sanity.

My favourite thing as a teenager was reading. I began my love affair with literature when I was thirteen or so by reading The Old Man and the Sea by Ernest Hemmingway. I was so smitten by the book that I sought out other Hemmingway stories but I lived on a remote island and so I couldn't find anything straight away and I began reading Graham Greene novels instead. I loved exploring these imaginary worlds, learning about human behaviour and drives through fiction, and so I kept on reading with an obsessiveness that only a teenage boy can bring to bear on his hobby. I was reading when I began pulling out my hair and the greatest tragedy of my life back then was that I could no longer sit still with a book because I would always pull hair when reading. I would switch between aesthetic joy on the one hand and self-loathing on the other and I can honestly say that hair pulling destroyed my love of literature and of life itself back then. I used to sit in a comfy chair in the corner of our living room and pull hairs out one after the other, sometimes stopping to look at the root or to pick the root off my finger if the gelatinous cylinder got stuck there. I dropped the hairs on the carpet by my side thinking

I would pick them all up and put them in the bin when I was finished reading so as to destroy the evidence. I usually remembered to do this.

I was scared about telling my parents what I was doing for many reasons. For one thing, I suspected that I was probably going a bit crazy and that I might need professional help, and this scared me. I wasn't mature enough to deal with it at all. My relationship with my dad was also a challenging one and I was scared to tell him in case he got angry with me. My dad was quite intense, and this usually manifested in clever and argumentative monologue; however, there were times when he would fly off the handle and I would feel wounded by his anger. I guess either I was far too sensitive or perhaps I hadn't developed a thick enough skin. I don't recall the order of events exactly, whether questions had been raised about my evidently thinning hair or not by this stage, but one day I was in the kitchen with my mum and my dad came storming through from the living room with a fist full of my hair.

'What is this?' he shouted. 'There are loads of hairs on the carpet next to that chair you've been reading in. What's going on?' He was clearly very upset.

I felt relieved in many ways because I knew that I had to tell my parents so that I could get some help but I had been scared of telling them. Quietly I said, 'I've been pulling it out.'

'What?'

'I've been pulling it out, and I can't stop. I don't know why.'

'No, you've not', he said with a smile and a shake of his head, when he recognized that I was feeling vulnerable. 'You can't have pulled all this hair out. You might think you've been pulling it out but it's a medical condition called alopecia.'

I couldn't believe it. I had told the truth and my dad didn't believe me. I felt so angry at him but my anger was drowned by a sea of sadness. I had told the truth and my parents should really have taken me at face value even if they weren't able to believe it at that stage. My dad said I should go to the doctor and the doctor would be able to tell me all about alopecia, and that they might be able to give me something for it. I said that it wasn't alopecia; that I really was pulling it out myself, but it took a long time for my dad to believe this.

One night he said that I couldn't be pulling my own hair out because it would hurt too much. I told him that it didn't hurt when I did it. I think he was still holding on to his idea that I was deluding myself; that my hair was actually falling out of its own accord. He asked me to pull one of his hairs out. It was funny. He was lying in bed watching TV. I didn't really want to pull one of his hairs out because I knew that it would hurt him, but I wanted to demonstrate that I had been telling the truth at the same time. I needed him to accept that I was pulling my hair out and so I stepped up to the plate, wound my fingers around one of his hairs and gave it a yank.

'Ouch!' he cried.

His pain made me feel better. I don't know what it made him feel but when I left his room I knew that my dad had to accept my explanation for my thinning hair.

I don't recall my mum's initial reaction but she told her hairdresser I was pulling out my hair and that I was scared to go to get it cut. The hairdresser had said not to worry, just to come in, and that another woman in the village did the same thing, too. This news did not encourage me, it made me squirm and feel very awkward. I was embarrassed on behalf of my mum for talking about this stuff with the hairdresser, and I was even embarrassed for the hairdresser because I imagined how horrified she would have been by the disclosure. For my hair pulling to be made public was awful because now the cat was out of the bag there was no longer any control over who knew about my shameful habit. I didn't like being lumped together with a sad woman from the village who shared my problem. The whole thing was just awful. I stayed away from the hairdresser even longer and by now my hair was starting to look suspicious. I had a big fringe that was hiding bald spots and I really needed a cut before I started looking like I was from a 1970s punk band. I was paranoid all the time. In the end, I did go to the hairdresser my mum had talked to, but I never said anything about pulling my hair and neither did the woman who cut my hair. Nevertheless, as I sat there I was so vigilant about being asked that my anxiety was through the roof. I had had a shower that morning and the hairdresser asked me casually if I had washed my hair. For some reason I thought you were not supposed to wash your hair before a haircut so I panicked and said no. How awkward.

After that, I tried different hairdressers and barbers in the village because I was so embarrassed about being known as a hair puller at the salon my mum went to, but I was fighting a losing battle because day by day, week by week, and month by month, I was sliding away from the comfort of having what appeared to be a normal head of hair into the realm of visibility, with obvious patches of hair loss. I was also steadily deforesting my legs and the rest of my body as well. Yet I tried to act with dignity while all the time I was burning with shame, hatred and confusion. They were the worst of times.

I don't remember well how I got on at school between the end of the exams and the summer break. We had a few weeks of classes where we started on the next year's courses before we broke up for summer. My guess is that I ignored the problem as best I could. In the summer holiday I worked in the bakery with my dad. I had to wear a hat so this covered up any bald spots while I was there. I do remember having to take the walk of shame from the door to the storeroom where I kept my hat and apron; I would have to do this every morning on my way in and every afternoon when I finished work. Nobody ever said anything but I felt self-conscious anyway. My dad knew that I was pulling my hair and I knew he wasn't very discrete. He told me some time over the next year that he had talked to the doctor about me and that I should go along myself and make an appointment. He also said he had talked to my guidance teacher at school.

I was so embarrassed and ashamed, I felt I could

just curl up and die. I skulked about wondering who

knew about my shame, waiting for socially awkward

things to happen. So by this stage I was dealing with

a new habit, loss of control over the habit, low self-

esteem and paranoia. Looking back I don't know

how I made it through each day; it must have been

exhausting.

Late in the summer holidays I got my exam results. I

did well, and I felt very proud and pleased with

myself. My parents were really happy for me. My

best friend and rival at school had got ever so

slightly lower marks than me so I was secretly

delighted to have got the best profile of results out

of all the kids in my year. But I was also terrified of myself and getting more and more scared about the future. One of the things on my mind when I had begun pulling was the future. I was studying hard for my exams as an investment in my future but I was seriously doubtful that I would be able to find love and have a family when I grew up and left home. So what was the point? I had always had body image problems since I was a child with eczema, and I was fat and depressed, and stressed with studying, and it all got too much for me. I snapped and began pulling my hair. Perhaps if I hadn't pulled my hair I would have had a breakdown, yet here I was with the grades to get into university but without any clear direction or hope for the future. I was a crisis waiting to happen.

In my final year at school I was elected Head Boy, which meant I had to be visible around the school. I had to walk round the school grounds and check that the prefects were doing what they were supposed to be doing, and the bald patches in my hair shifted more slowly than clouds in the sky but faster than continental drift. Every day when I talked to people I would try to maintain eye contact so that I would know whether people were looking at my hair. I burned with shame wherever I went. Boys and girls were getting together romantically increasingly often. The air was filled with a potent mix of hormones and sexual possibility yet I felt cut off from it. I stood apart; I was strange and unlovable. I was so happy to get home from school each day, away from public scrutiny. At least at home my family knew my secret so I could let my guard down a little lower, though of course there were tensions at home as well.

I found it very difficult to decide what to study at university. My greatest interest was literature and all I wanted was to study literature with the hope that I might become a writer someday. My dad was dead set against the idea. He wanted me to study something that would translate my good grades into a high income career. He once claimed that he had talked to teachers at the school and they would be disappointed if I studied English rather than accountancy or medicine. I didn't believe my teachers had said any such thing to him. It was amazing the lengths he went to. I remember arguing with him about it endlessly in the kitchen after school and in the evenings. The only fall-back position after studying literature, in his mind, was to become a school teacher, and he thought I should be able to do better for myself than that. I wanted material success; don't get me wrong, it was part of my dreams of becoming a writer. In my mind I wanted to escape the daily grind by writing a bestseller and selling the movie rights. But I also dreamed about academic success. I had read that Friedrich Nietzsche had got a doctoral degree by the age of 25 and I dreamed about doing one better than that. My ambitions were clearly not restricted to money. In the end my dad won the argument; my ego was not strong enough to keep fighting for what

I wanted. I went to a reputable university to study law. I did have an interest in justice and I hoped that would sustain me, but when I got there one day I canvassed opinion on why some other students had opted to study law and they all mentioned the money. I was the only person primarily interested in justice. It added to the feeling that I was out of place at law school.

Just as I turned eighteen I found myself living in a student residence in a small, Spartan room next door to a religious boy who had been a year ahead of me at school. I didn't know anybody else there. I was so shy that I only went to eat in the dining room once because it overwhelmed me. I hid in my room and went to my classes and then came home and hid in my room again. I went to church with the guy next door one Sunday but all they preached was supplication to an angry God and I felt alienated. In my mind God was love. I grew increasingly angry at my circumstances in life. Why was I marked out for this terrible affliction? I walked through those halls with several bald patches on my scalp and I felt so self-conscious and lonely. I felt that I just wasn't up to scratch. For a short time at university I got engaged in my studies but every time I got my head down in my books at the library I found myself pulling more and more hair out. I felt deep shame. I was embarrassed that I might be observed pulling out my hair. Inevitably I left the library with some work remaining to be done.

I turned up late for one of my exams shortly before the Christmas holidays. I only realised that I was late when I got to the exam hall and found that everybody was inside already. I had noted down the time incorrectly and I had to sit the paper in the lecturer's room straight away afterwards. I felt stupid. I felt miles away from the boy who had done so well at school. Over Christmas I convinced my parents that I should move out of halls and into a shared flat with a friend, and they reluctantly agreed. Over the next few months, every night I went to bed with plans to go in to university and have a productive day and every morning I woke up and reset my alarm clock. I eventually stopped going to class altogether and then I failed my exams.

My hair looked very odd and one day when I did actually make it into class one of the cool, fashion-conscious boys on my course said, 'You have the weirdest hair I have ever seen'. I tried my best to laugh and shrug it off. I went to a barber's shop and the guy asked me what was going on with my hair. He had a disgusted look on his face. I acted ignorant and said I didn't know. He told me I should probably go and get checked out by a doctor.

One day my friend bought some clippers and gave me a short buzz cut. It was a revelation because it made my hair too short to pull. That day was the first time I hadn't pulled hair out of my scalp for over a year. I still pulled hair out from my body every day. I pulled from my legs when I sat on the toilet, and from the rest of my body when lying in bed at night and first thing on awakening the next morning. Pulling from my body wasn't as much of a problem for me because nobody ever really saw my body. I had no sex life to worry about. I lived in a country without much sunny weather so I never had to wear shorts. It was easy to masquerade as a real person as long as I kept my hair short.

Life went on like this for years. I tried a different course at university. I failed a year and then did it again. I began drinking socially and going out to house clubs, where I danced for hours to the new electronic music coming out of Detroit and Chicago. I found a kind of happiness and a community to belong to, yet the two things I longed for were still as far away as ever. I craved intimacy with a woman, and I wanted to write a novel more than ever. I got close to a few women but always pushed them away, usually by failing to read the signs that they might be interested in me. I hadn't told anybody about pulling my hair and I was convinced any woman would think I was a freak so I didn't dare allow myself become vulnerable. I dropped out of university and had time on my hands where I might have written my novel. But I was on the run from myself. I was on the run from my feelings, which were too terrible to bear. I was on the run from my parents, who I tried to fool into thinking I was doing okay and making progress at university during our weekly phone calls. I kept running until I couldn't run any longer and I had to go home and tell my parents I wasn't coping with life.

My last year in the city trying to get a degree at this stage of my life had been a disaster from the start. I don't recall whether it was social anxiety related to bald spots that stopped me making it into class or if it was depression. Maybe it doesn't even matter because they were two parts of the same problem. In any case, I flunked out of a Gaelic course after a matter of weeks at the beginning of the autumn semester, and the realisation that I had failed once again to make my way through university made me give up completely. I dropped out of courses one after the other so that by the time exams came round in the summer I lied to everyone and pretended to sit them when in fact I had dropped out completely by that stage. It is bad enough lying to your parents, it's quite another thing to lie to your friends who provided a network of social support that just about kept my head above water. I felt guilty as hell and was having difficulty finding the motivation to go on living. These were very dark times. I was in my early twenties and part of me was ready to slip quietly into the nearest grave.

It was time to face facts because I couldn't go on running any more. I wasn't functioning. But now it felt like that mask was slipping and the depression was about to swallow me up. The year was painful for me on many levels. I reached out for love and crumbled when I realised how terribly scared I was;

how sure I was of rejection. I hated myself so how could I have expected anybody else to love me? I failed to engage in creative writing despite telling myself that that was how I would spend my time profitably after dropping out of university. My pulling got worse and worse. I often found myself sitting up into the small hours pulling fistfuls of hair out from my body, lamenting my lot in life. I got into debt and dwelt on Hamlet's dilemma.

When I got home I knew it was only a matter of time before my parents would expect exam results. I rehearsed in my head what I would say to them when I plucked up the courage, but that courage never came and I sank deeper into depression. I spent a lot of time reading T.S Eliot's poem Ash

Wednesday and I wept uncontrollably. I could feel the abyss. One day I wrote a letter to my parents setting out my realisation that I had flunked out of university, had an unsurmountable problem with pulling my hair and that for some reason I could not understand I was destroying my life. I wrote that I wanted to get help for hair pulling, and that I didn't feel able to move forward with my life until I had addressed my psychological problems. It was a hard letter to write, but putting it all into a letter was easier than starting a conversation because I felt so ashamed of my failure and weakness. I left the letter on the kitchen table and went out for a drive. When I came home hours later there was a letter waiting for me written by my dad. He expressed how sorry he was that I was having these problems, and that I felt I couldn't talk to him. When I saw him he hugged me, and so did my mum. It was a small but reassuring relief. I no longer had to hide from my parents but I still had hair pulling and a mood disorder to deal with.

I had read a newspaper article describing compulsive hair pulling as a form of Obsessive-Compulsive Disorder. I went to see the doctor and told him I suspected I had OCD. I told the doctor that I couldn't stop pulling my hair out and that I couldn't sleep at night. He gave me some anti-depressant medicine and referred me to see a clinical psychologist. He asked me to come back after a week to check in with him. The pills helped me. For the first time in years I dropped off into a sound sleep. I spent the week soberly, quietly, reflecting on the low point I was living through.

I only took the pills for a few weeks. I started to feel much better after unburdening myself to my parents. I had to wait a long time to get an appointment with the clinical psychologist, and in that time I met a girl who kept my head above water. Unfortunately I wasn't able to share my secrets with her; I wasn't able to be truly intimate. I think she saw the sadness in me, and I suspected that after a while she knew there was something wrong with my hair. I thought I kept seeing her looking at my strange hairline but I couldn't bring myself to ask her. I stayed numb. I didn't know if I was being paranoid or not but I just knew that if I lifted the lid of my emotions with her I might lose myself completely. I was too raw and afraid to take a risk at that time and so I ended up acting like a dick and letting her down. I still feel guilty about it to this day. From time to time I am consumed with the desire to tell her that it was all my fault, that I was having problems at the time, and that she had saved me in her way. But our paths don't cross very frequently, and in any case it is a long time ago now.

Because I lived on a remote island my first appointment with the clinical psychologist was done via video link from a room in the local hospital. This mode of communication added to the strangeness of the experience. I sat down in front of a screen and had a conversation with a disembodied head.

The woman on the other side of the screen seemed very empathetic, and spoke with a priestly air. It felt like I was in confession. She asked me some questions about hair pulling and my general circumstances but I felt very shy talking to her and didn't make the most of the situation. She told me I could write to her if that was easier so that is what I did before the next appointment. I sat down and poured my grief into a letter, describing my woes and the possible reasons for my hair pulling as I understood them. At the second appointment she was better informed and asked me to keep a diary of my hair pulling over a week. She wanted to know where I was when I pulled, how much I pulled and where from, and what I was thinking about at the time. I kept the diary diligently for about two and a half days before I saw that each day's pattern was the same. I pulled at every opportunity I had. I wasn't really thinking much while I pulled but when I noticed I was pulling I loathed myself.

After a few remote video-mediated sessions, she asked me to travel to have my next appointment in person. I drove for about a couple of hours to the nearest big town, where clinical psychology was based in a new wing at the renowned psychiatric facility. This psychiatric unit was famous for everybody where I lived. As children we would taunt each other about having to go there. The clinical psychologist had given me directions to take a left turn and drive up the hill to the hospital. I was quite anxious when driving through, for all sorts of reasons, and one of the things on my mind was that I didn't know the way and that I had to get there on time. Eventually I saw a sign for the hospital and noticed it was immediately before a break in the fence, so I indicated, slowed right down, and then turned off the busy road. I found myself driving up the hill in the direction of the hospital on an old farm track. The track wasn't too bad so I decided to continue on up the hill rather than try to reverse onto the busy road. Unfortunately, as I drove up the track the grass got longer and longer until the tyre tracks disappeared completely. I had such a dilemma, but I thought I would just plough on regardless. At the top of the hill I scraped the undercarriage of the car off a herbaceous border and raced across a small plot of grass onto the hospital carpark. I thought if you are going to travel to a psychiatric facility you might as well do it in style.

I think I stopped making appointments. I guess I was too immature for therapy at this stage. But life began to evolve slowly. I had a friend who worked for a company that trained people to become English language teachers and she encouraged me to get away from home and put my mind to some good use. I really liked this girl, and although things had never worked out between us I still hoped they might. She lived in Spain. We hatched a plan for me to do the training course in England and then go to Spain to teach and learn Spanish. We talked about going away to travel round South America together and the part of me that often said fuck it said 'Fuck it, let's do it!' I applied and was accepted but the next course was filled up already and I had to wait about six months until the next one. I stayed home and kept on trying to keep my head above water.

THE ROAD TO ROUEN

In the months before I left for England I met a girl.

She was fun and clever and extremely beautiful and

we struck up a rapport quite naturally. She was way

out of my league physically and she was also young.

She had just left high school and was waiting to

begin university at the end of the summer. I was a

twenty-four year old derelict at the time. I couldn't

help but talk to her whenever I saw her. She was

attractive and we had fun. I never went into it

thinking seriously that we might get together but in

the end we did. I let her get closer to me than anybody before but I was still unable to tell her my shameful secret. We began to see each other more and more, and we even pronounced love for each other after a while, but because I hadn't been fully honest with her I believed that she didn't really love me. I beat myself up for being dishonest with her. I told myself that if I told her about my hair-pulling she would be disgusted and want nothing to do with me. So these were difficult days. I was half in love and half in fear. I was feeling confident and doubtful. I was happy and sad. Yet, as always, part of me kept pushing her away.

I got a job teaching English in a language school in a small city in northern France. This was only around eighteen months after my lowest ebb when I moved home and sought psychological help. I thought there was a good chance that I would be on a plane heading home after a shambolic week or two. However, I also took strength from my ability to get through the training course pretty well, and from my new girlfriend overlooking things that I considered to be shortcomings such as my eczema and being overweight. I was beginning to have a little more faith in myself after a very rough few years.

In the end I did get on okay at the job. I found my feet teaching and really enjoyed the experience. I had always had a strong work ethic and this came out at the school. I got a little studio apartment in a modern block near the city centre. My girlfriend came over to spend the summer with me. They were blissful times. We lived happily together for several weeks, with me spending long days working of course. I was still paranoid about physical intimacy in case she noticed the sparseness of the hair on my body. I hated wearing shorts when we were out and about in the warm summer weather. I avoided going swimming. My hair also grew quite long while I was there because I didn't have any clippers and I was unsure what to ask for at a French barber's. My bald patches grow in quite well when I maintain short hair but whenever I leave the hair to grow longer I inevitably begin to pull it out and have to try desperately to check myself. The only thing I have found to stop me pulling is to get up and do a different activity, which of course sucks if you are trying to read a book or do some writing.

After the summer when my girlfriend had returned to university one of the other teachers I spent a lot of my social time with left and I began spending more time alone. My hair was still long and I was pulling more and more of it out, leaving some balding patches. I got toothache and I fell into a depression. I was mostly concerned with the problem of telling my girlfriend I pulled my hair. I was scared she would fall out of love with me; in fact, I was certain that would happen, if not because she was disgusted then because I had failed to tell her the truth. I wrote a letter to my parents telling them something of my dilemma. My mum took a flight out to see me the next weekend and I booked us a hotel in Paris. We didn't talk about it until the morning she was leaving. I have always found it a difficult thing to bring up so it was left to my brave mother. She said she wouldn't think it awfully bad if a guy told a girl that he pulled out his hair. I felt cynically that she was only saying that because she was my mother. In truth, whenever I have listened to my heart I have believed that another loving person would accept my hair-pulling but that hasn't stopped me being scared. Nor has it stopped my mind from racing. Over the next few weeks my toothache got worse and I decided to quit my job and return home to tell my girlfriend my secret.

So there has been a lot of water under the bridge

between my return from France until the time of writing this tale. I made my awkward confession to the girl, she was amazingly cool about it. I decided to give university another shot and I finally got a degree, and then another. I got married and we bought a place to live. In fact, we have moved twice since then, and now we live in a nice house on top of a little hill in a nice neighbourhood. I have forged a career in scientific research. We have begun a family. On the surface, therefore, life is sweet. Yet I remain gripped by trichotillomania, and every time I let my hair grow too long I begin pulling it out, and I have to face all my old demons again. I am sick and tired of it.

SONG OF EXPERIENCE

When I finally made a success of university I studied

psychology. I learned a lot about the laws that

govern learning, such as classical and operant

conditioning. What I learned allowed me to infer

that I get rewarded for pulling hair out by the

release of chemicals in the brain. These chemicals

are addictive. My inability to stop myself from

pulling out hair is due to the strength of the

association between pulling hairs and the reward it

provides me with. Please note that this is all my own

thinking and not hard-cast verifiable scientific observation.

I have talked to a series of clinicians and therapists over the years and some of them have helped me, but so far I have been unable to exert control over the disorder. I live happily enough by keeping my hair cropped short, and usually manage to get a haircut in time before falling into the abyss. Recently I have been thinking a bit differently about this disorder, and I have asked myself whether I should just learn to live with trichotillomania as a part of my life or whether 'defeating' it is actually possible. I still don't know the answer. The best thing that professionals have been able to do for me so far is help me to accept that hair pulling is just a thing that I do. It is such a small part of my life that it doesn't define who I am. It is easy to believe in this line of thought in my day to day life, as I juggle work and family commitments, yet whenever my behaviour gets out of control and I am conscious of having bald spots on my scalp I feel determined that I want to find a cure. I want to remove this unwanted and destructive house guest from my life because they have overstayed their welcome.

There are many stories out there of people who have stopped pulling their hair, and this gives me some hope that I can do it too. Yet, so far I have been unable to help myself stop. I am now officially middle aged by anyone's standards, and I believe it is more difficult to make changes to your life as you get older. William James, brother of the famous

novelist Henry James and the great grand-daddy of

psychology, believed that our behaviour is set in

stone by the age of thirty. This doesn't give me

much hope, but hope is a tenuous thing and mine

hasn't snuffed out completely.

Over the past few years I have been talking with a

psychotherapist once a week. I pay her so that I can

sit in her office and spill my guts for an hour. She

listens and helps me to understand myself. It has

been quite weird but very useful. My therapist

thinks that the roots of my trichotillomania lie much

deeper than the set of circumstances I found myself

in when revising for my 5th year exams. Looking

back from today's perspective, I do suspect that I

was depressed for much of my early teenage years. I was a boy struggling with over-eating and with extreme self-consciousness. Indeed, I remember feeling ashamed and embarrassed on my first day in primary school when I brought in a cup of juice to drink when all my classmates were given milk. My parents thought that I might be allergic to dairy products so I wasn't allowed to have the free milk that was given to all of the pupils in the class. I felt self-conscious about it, even at the age of four. I also remember that we had little cards with our names on them set out on the tables and that one of the girls' dads swapped my card with his daughter's so that she could sit next to her friend. Nobody noticed him swapping the names except for me. I was worried that I would get in trouble for sitting in the wrong seat. The swap also meant that I was sitting at the end of a row next to only one person rather than sitting between two people. I sat down to begin my education with a cup of juice brought in from home next to a girl who ignored me and chatted to her friend. This is what I remember about my first day at school. I wonder what an analyst would make of the four year old me. It is possible that the seeds of my future problems were sown by this time, which is a view that conforms to the model of personality development that my therapist uses.

I have lots of different snapshot memories from early childhood. It is hard to say if I was happy or sad. I guess I went through the normal range of emotions and was both happy and sad at times. I remember being sad and angry and frustrated with my skin, and having arguments with my parents when they told me to stop scratching. Today I see scratching my skin as a similar behaviour to pulling my hair, with the only real difference being that scratching can be viewed as a direct consequence of itchy skin and therefore a natural thing. It has never been so clear to me that hair pulling might be just as natural. However, at some stage I obviously learned to scratch too much, and that an analgesic release from pain could be brought about by scratching so much that addictive neurotransmitters are released. I remember crying and scratching and feeling like I was getting a row for scratching, being told that I just had to get used to it. Maybe there I learned to blunt my emotional response, to keep my troubles to myself. Perhaps in that moment I cursed god for my lot in life. It is hard to say.

The therapeutic process is helpful but slow and bewildering. I was quickly diagnosed with poor emotional intelligence, which makes total sense now but came as a bit of a shock at the time. I'm British after all. I come from the country that champions a stiff upper lip. I now understand that I may fail to process emotional material in a healthy way, and that I need to allow my feelings to take their natural course before I can move on. One part of the therapy has involved recognising that I tend to block my emotional response to negative events in my life and so I have been trying hard to feel emotions as they arise and let them dissipate.

Previously, I had the habit of resisting a full

experience of negative emotion, which drives the

emotion underground where it festers. (Okay, this

Freudian model doesn't sit well with what I have

learned as a student of psychology. But it's my

therapist's model so for the time being I am trying

to suspend judgment and just run with it). I have

always had a very long fuse, but I do end up getting

tetchier and tetchier over time if negative events

accumulate. It does not sit easily with me to allow

myself feel anger, to follow a negative thought, to

suffer a negative emotion, but I have been getting

better at it. It also feels true that a negative emotion

experienced fully will dissipate after a short time,

which is preferable to the lengthy periods of

negativity bubbling away beneath the surface that I was used to previously. Still, it is not a natural thing for me to do. My therapist seems to want me to have arguments with people, but I would still rather shy away from confrontation and use logic to solve all my problems. It is funny and strange. I sometimes think that I might be a Vulcan trapped in a human body.

Aside from improving my emotional intelligence, my therapist also believes that I need to allow my inner child to decide not to hurt myself in response to my perception that the world is unfair because I have eczema. I laughed the first time she mentioned the inner child. I thought 'Here we go, next stop California.' But the idea that the ego contains child, adult and parent states seems like a reasonable metaphor to me now. Again, I think if it's useful then let's roll with it.

I don't have access to any early trauma other than eczema so I hope and pray that it is the root of my trichotillomania. The therapist's idea is that some early trauma happened to me, and that this has led to eczema, over-eating, depression, trichotillomania, etc. So maybe my journey down the birth canal was a bit bumpy, or I was allergic to cow's milk, or whatever. Something could have happened when I was so young that I don't have access to any memory of it, and this something might be the seed of my struggle with hair pulling. One of the problems here is that research has shown that this type of scrambling about in the unknown recesses of the mind can lead to the construction of false memories. Elizabeth Loftus' research demonstrates this clearly. So obviously, in undergoing therapy, I worry that some other kind of buried trauma may be constructed and blamed for my woes. I guard against it.

I think that the experience of eczema is a sufficient cause of trichotillomania in my case. The pain and emotional turmoil it causes me could in themselves have allowed me develop self-limiting beliefs and habits. Obviously, not every person with eczema gets trichotillomania, so there must be some aspect of my personality that comes in to play, too. I can also see a direct link between scratching and hair pulling, yet there is an additional element to trichotillomania that I believe I need to explore. What I mean to say is that trichotillomania has a dissociative element to it. When I began to suffer from trichotillomania something snapped within me and I developed the thousand yard stare so often linked with combat veterans. In any case, according to my therapist I need to try to experience the childhood emotional states I should have processed correctly back when other kids took the piss out of my skin, or when I cried and scratched in response to my parents telling me to stop scratching. My therapist thinks that there is a kernel of self-destructive anger in my primitive emotional response that still may be at play today when I lose myself to hair pulling. I want to explore it but my memory for these early events is so patchy that it is mostly guesswork. So for the time being I am patiently waiting for my inner child to decide to stop pulling my hair out. All the while, my emotional and financial resources are running out.

Sigmund Freud's work on subconscious drives is widely criticized by modern scientists, and Freud is barely even mentioned to students taking an undergraduate degree in psychology any more. His work is sniggered at. Today, we don't like theories that concern things we cannot measure. How can you measure the extent of somebody's Oedipus complex, or their latent homosexuality? While we have been waiting for the answers to these questions, science has moved on. We live in a world

where Cognitive Behavioural Therapy is widely
championed, because it provides us with
measurements of things like anxiety and depression.
It is routinely shown that CBT leads to a reduction in
the symptoms of mild to moderate depression, for
example. This modern therapeutic approach doesn't
care much about childhood trauma. It doesn't
require people to root about in the dark of their
subconscious minds. It is in fact a very useful tool
for helping people to challenge how they think
about things and to modify their behaviour
accordingly. It's like a good dose of philosophy.

Getting access to CBT is no easy thing in the UK. The
National Health Service is chronically under-
resourced. British people demand first class medical

care but politicians don't want to put up taxes to pay for it. Therefore, there are lengthy waiting lists for people who need to see a clinical psychologist. CBT in its barest form can be offered to people via computer or in group sessions by trained clinicians who are not necessarily fully qualified clinical psychologists. According to the small amount of research that has been conducted, it seems that a type of CBT called Habit Reversal Training is the best option for treating trichotillomania. From what I understand, this training involves learning to make a new response every time you feel the urge to pull your hair. The new response is incompatible with pulling out a hair, so might be something along the lines of making a fist. I have been trying for years to find a therapist who can offer habit reversal training and who has a track record with treating trichotillomania but I am starting to believe that there is nobody within travelling distance who can help me. Maybe it is time to help myself.

The exact choice of therapeutic approach to treating trichotillomania is therefore mixed. Methods derived from CBT offer the most promise for helping people to re-learn their bad habits, but can be criticized for not looking under the hood to see exactly why people develop the disorder in the first place. More traditional forms of talking therapy may help people discover why they have developed certain personality traits but do not focus squarely enough on the specific problem of hair pulling. For me, I think both approaches have merit, and while I am doing well in general terms with psychotherapy I feel I need to work at the other end on habit reversal as well.

Lately I have been embracing my inner hippie. Maybe it's the result of some kind of mid-life crisis, or maybe it's just the right thing for me to do, but in any case it has helped me an awful lot on my journey from feeling like a freak to believing we all have something unique to offer the world. I came down with depression a few years ago and spent a while reading up on ways to help myself get better. Most of the advice I read included some mention of meditation, mostly as a device that can be used to quieten the mind and let you take a break from the constant negative thoughts that accompany depressed mood. So I read up on meditation and gave it a try. There are some guided mediations you can listen to on the internet so I tried some of them. However, each one has a different spiritual slant to it. The descriptions often talk about how you can use the meditation to open up your chakras, and other such exotic claims which do not sit well with my Presbyterian background. Even from my psychology degree I am aware of mindfulness and how it is touted as a panacea for mental health problems. Mindfulness is basically just secularised Buddhism, as far as I can tell. So I read up on mindfulness and gave it a shot, too. And then I came upon a great website called Tiny Buddha (http://tinybuddha.com/), which publishes brief, upbeat articles about how to live well. The site offers ethics for the modern age. Most of the articles talked about the benefit of compassion, for oneself and for others.

Taking all of this research on board, I have been trying to lead a more compassionate life, and I believe it has contributed to my recovery from depression. I know that being mean to myself is neither fun nor helpful. I work hard to counter my inner critic and to be kind to myself. This seems to be particularly important whenever I start to pull out my hair. It helps me to limit the amount of hair that I pull out, and to decrease the amount of time I might spend in the type of negative frame of mind that often leads to bad episodes. Inherent to trying to live a compassionate life is self-acceptance.

Maybe the cure for trichotillomania looks different from what I have long hoped for. Maybe the best I should hope for is to limit the negative impact that this disorder has on my life. I've been living with trichotillomania for most of my life by now, and on the whole my life is good.

IT'S JUST A THING THAT I DO

The best online resource for trichotillomania that I have come across is the Trichotillomania Learning Center (http://www.trich.org), which is run from California in the USA. This non-profit organization provides education and supports research into body-focused repetitive disorders. The TLC holds conferences and invites researchers and clinicians to talk to attendees, who are typically people who struggle with trichotillomania and their families. These conferences have been on my radar for a few years now and I have often thought about travelling

across the Atlantic Ocean to go to one of them.

Money and opportunity have stood in my way, but

more than these constraints I have felt uneasy

about the prospect of immersing myself in such a

community. Until a few months ago I had never

spoken to a single person who also pulled their hair

in the way that I do. I wondered what actual benefit

there would be in sitting in a conference hall with

other miserable people.

This summer I went to a TLC meeting in London. It

was the first time they had held an event in the UK

and the opportunity to attend was too good to miss.

In reality, I think that the work that I have been

doing recently with my therapist on understanding

my emotions better was key to my decision to go to this meeting. Even last year I don't think I could have gone to a similar type of event. I just wasn't ready for it. But this summer, it felt right and so I flew down to London early one Saturday morning and made my way to a lecture theatre in King's College.

There were two great talks by a psychiatrist from Chicago called Jon Grant, who covered the history of the disorder and outlined the research base that informs our current understanding of body focused repetitive disorders like hair pulling, skin picking, and nail biting. There were also two very moving talks by Suzanne Mouton-Odum, a psychologist from Houston who treats people that struggle with trichotillomania in her clinic.

It was strange to sit in a room with other people like me. I was nervous but took some comfort from being part of a group of people who share similar struggles. With my cropped hair I felt relatively incognito, as if I could have been a researcher or a therapist rather than one of them: a hair puller. I sat and looked at the other people in front of me while listening to the talks. Some people couldn't keep their hands away from their scalp for very long. Other people wore wigs or hats. Others still were missing their eye lashes. I thought that we were all very brave to come together in this way, to tacitly accept that we are part of this same tragic struggle.

74

I believe that the way forward for me is to live my life compassionately. When I can quieten down the incessant chatter of my mind and dig deep within myself I find that I have a compassionate heart. I know that I feel so much compassion for my family and my friends but I haven't always been compassionate to myself.

Sometimes I tell myself terrible things. I tell myself that I'm a great, big loser and that I am subhuman because of hair pulling. But even before I began to pull out my hair I think I failed to love myself enough. I hated my skin and cursed my lot in life as a young child. Was it any wonder that I began tearing at my hair when experiencing stress as a teenager?

I was particularly moved by Suzanne Mouton-Odum's words at the TLC workshop. Her key message was that trichotillomania in itself isn't that big a thing. People with the disorder should tell themselves that it is just a thing that they do in order to regulate their systems. Most people have something that they do to relieve stress or to focus their energies. Some people bite their nails; other people develop ticks. Some people use alcohol; other people smoke or eat too much. Some people gamble; others use drugs. Some people get addicted to shopping or to sex. Compulsive hair pulling is just a thing people do. When we experience shame or self-loathing because of hair pulling it just doesn't help. It makes things worse.

Over the years I have allowed hair pulling affect my life negatively, but I really believe now that I need to make a truce with the disorder in order to move on with my life. Yes, I pull my hair out when I wish I didn't, but I will no longer allow this peccadillo erode the positive regard that I hold for myself. Life is too short, and on balance I am too awesome.

If you struggle with trichotillomania then please be kind to yourself. Please try to practise compassion. I can assure you that it helps. If you struggle with anything at all that life has to offer, from across the wide and varied range of mental health and social problems, then please work at placing compassion for yourself and for others at the centre of your life. Compassion is the key to contentment.

Namaste.

Q & A

1. Why do you pull out your hair?

I really don't know. I suppose I do it because it feels good. For some bizarre reason it is just strangely satisfying. The trichotillomania label is very apt because there is a certain mania to be experienced when in a bout of hair pulling.

2. How exactly does hair pulling make you feel?

If I give free reign to hair pulling it makes me feel a crazy joy. It is energising and compelling and it provides a high in much the same way as drugs, sex, sport or shopping can, depending on your particular predilections. Hair pulling is so enjoyable for me that it is often the pain I begin to feel in my fingertips from repetitive activity that serves to bring my mind to what I am doing and what the consequences of the behaviour might be. At times, I have pulled until both my scalp is bleeding and my hand is cramped, and I would continue pulling if only I could. Such is the addictive nature of compulsive hair pulling.

3. Why can't you just stop after pulling one or two hairs?

It is extremely difficult to exert conscious control over the behaviour. I have battled and willed myself to stop but it seems just impossible to control myself. It is incredibly frustrating. Sometimes I say to myself, 'Okay just one more hair', and I try to focus on pulling the hair out and having a little look at the root and then disposing of the hair and getting on with whatever I was trying to do before being interrupted by trichotillomania. And then I find, perhaps just seconds later, that I have begun to pull hair out again. Sometimes I keep a hold of the hair I have just pulled so that my hands are not free to pull another hair. Yet, even then, I end up dropping that hair and pulling more out. It is as if my mind has become split between one side that is

horrified by my hair pulling habit and is conscious of

the damage I am doing both to my hair and to

myself, and then there is another side of me who

efficiently pulls out hair after hair and feels exalted

by the feeling it provides. It is terrifying when you

become conscious of this split. It really makes me

wonder what part of me is in charge, and makes me

worry that I am weak willed.

4. Isn't it sore?

No. Hair pulling usually doesn't hurt. I think it is

similar to tickling. You can't tickle yourself – try it.

When you are a compulsive hair puller you can't

hurt yourself either, or at least you are not in touch

with the pain.

5. What do you do with the hair?

I am a bit of a slob so for a long time I just tended to drop the hair on the floor. If I only pulled out a small number of hairs then I forgot about them but if I went on a spree and pulled lots out then I would do a walk of shame to the cupboard and get the hoover out. These days we have wooden floors in our living room and the hairs don't just disappear like they do in a carpet so I am more conscientious and tend to put the hairs in the bin. I have read that some people eat the hair, which to me seems like a strange thing to do. But of course, to someone who doesn't pull his or her hair out then what I do must seem very strange. So I do not judge people who eat their hair, I feel very sorry for them, particularly since I understand that big balls of hair can collect in the intestines and require medical attention. There but for the grace of god go I.

6. Do you pull hair out in front of other people or to get attention?

The last thing I want is attention from anybody when I pull hair out. I would burn with shame if I absent-mindedly pulled some hair out in public and somebody asked me what I was doing. I have often wondered if subconsciously I need to advertise something about myself to other people, like my craziness, or sadness, or simply a lack of reproductive fitness, but it is next to impossible to second guess what your subconscious motives might be. I have as much access to my subconscious drives as the next person. All I can say is that consciously, hair pulling has nothing to do with getting attention from other people. In fact, the opposite is true because what people who pull their hair out tend to do is to lock themselves away from other people, shunning family relationships and neglecting friendships because they are too ashamed of what they do to their hair in secret.

7. Where do you pull hair out from?

I pull hair out from all over my body: my scalp, my eyebrows, my stubble when it is long enough, my nose, my ears, my chest, my arms, my pubic hair, my bottom, my legs and my toes. Fortunately, I have never pulled out my eyelashes, and I shave if my stubble becomes long enough to pull. One time quite recently I lost almost an entire sideburn during a morning sitting at my desk. After an awkward train ride home, to balance it out I just shaved the other one off that night. The most damaging place to pull hair from is my scalp. Whenever my hair grows long enough I begin to pull it out. To avoid the dire social and emotional consequences of having bald spots I try to keep my hair short enough that I cannot readily pull it out. When I am at work I pull hair from my arms if my head hair is kept short. I am so thankful that most of the hair regrows because by now I would be completely hairless from head to toe if the hairs did not regenerate. Having said that, there are some places like on my legs where I don't have much hair, and on my head the area where I pulled most of my hair out has quite a lot of white hairs now. I guess with constant pulling and regrowth my hair is old before its time.

8. Is some hair better than others?

Yes, we have lots of different types of hair and some types of hair are better to pull out than others. Thick, twisted hairs are good to pull out, as are new hairs that are growing in to replace previously pulled hair. For me, the best thing is when I pull a hair that is growing over an area of skin that is inflamed or otherwise damaged. What I suspect is going on in the background is that different types of hair cause different amounts of damage, which in turn leads to variation in the amount of biochemical release in the brain. So thick hairs, for example, might lead to a larger amount of endorphin to be released than normal hair. Also when new hairs are pulled out more of the root comes out with them, so perhaps this greater area of tissue being plucked out from the scalp releases more endorphin than older hairs do. The relationship between types of hair and endorphin release is my own speculation, but it offers an explanation of why some hairs are more sought after than others.

9. Are there other behaviours that you cannot control?

Yes, I am compulsive in a number of other ways as well. I scratch my skin and pick at scabs in a compulsive manner. This has never really bothered me because until recently I always attributed it to eczema. Because I itch all the time there didn't seem to be anything pathological about it. I also eat

compulsively and as a consequence I am

overweight. This does bother me and I struggle to

eat sensibly and exercise enough. It is a battle that I

am not winning, though. Maybe lots of people who

are overweight are actually behaving compulsively.

Maybe psychological treatments should be more

readily available to combat obesity. Finally, I

sometimes keep my hands under hot water from

the tap as the temperature increases and increases

until I can't stand it. I assume that this provides me

with a similar biochemical release to hair pulling.

10. How do you feel in social situations when you have visible bald patches?

I die a thousand deaths inside whenever I have bald patches and I am in company. My stress is through the roof and I cannot remain in any public setting for very long. I become paranoid, convinced that everybody can see my strange head of hair and knows there is something not right about it. If I assume that people know I must pull my hair for it to look that way I feel terribly ashamed. If I assume that people can see something is wrong but do not consider that I pull my own hair out then I feel guilty. A friend once asked if I had had cancer a few years earlier when I had no choice but to let my bald patches be seen. I froze and burned with shame, denying any knowledge of what he was talking about. How terrible for people to think you have cancer when you have created the bald patches yourself. Okay, on one level I know that it is trichotillomania that causes my hair pulling behaviour, but on another level I blame myself for doing it, and of course I feel very guilty about it.

When I have bald patches I avoid socialising as much as I can. I never want to go out to meet friends when I have been pulling a lot of hair out because I am afraid of their questions. I am actually even afraid of their perceptions of me, which I think is paranoid and irrational. When forced to go out I used to be in the habit of wearing a hat, but the thing is I only ever wore a hat when I had bald patches and because I knew this the hats became a loud signal that I had been pulling my hair. To make matters worse, I go a bit crazy whenever I get too hot, which is an eczema thing, I believe. So when I wore a hat to hide bald patches I would heat up and wind up on top of everything else I was going through. Every moment spent in public with bald patches is extremely self-conscious and filled with self-loathing. I am brimming with intense negative emotion that I fight to keep down and I cannot wait to find sanctuary at home or in some other safe place where I am confident that nobody will come looking for answers.

11. Why do you feel so ashamed?

I feel so ashamed because my troubles seem to be of my own making. I pull my own hair out, there is nobody standing over me with a gun making me do it. I am the instrument of my own pain, and I do not have enough self-control to stop creating this crippling problem for myself over and over again. I don't feel ashamed of having eczema, even though it has caused some embarrassment over the years. For some biological reason my skin has a disease, and even though I pick at scabs and scratch my skin until it is badly inflamed, I do not blame myself. However, I do blame myself for pulling out my hair, and I do feel lacking as a human being because I cannot exert any control over myself.

12. Why can't you talk to friends about it?

I am so profoundly ashamed of myself that I cannot bring myself to talk to my friends about it. I would rather uncomfortable self-consciousness than full disclosure. I fear that my friends would not like me any more if I told them I pulled my hair out and that the scariest thing was that I couldn't stop doing it. I am scared by my own lack of self-control: I assume my friends would be scared, too. Plus, my friends are such a positive resource for me; they distract me from my shameful self and support and comfort me in a million ways. I dare not put my friendships in jeopardy for the sake of this small but critical secret.

13. Do you think you will ever stop?

My greatest fear is that I will never be able to move on from this awful habit, and that I will pull my hair out in a compulsive manner until the day I die.

Allied to this fear is the worry that my children may inherit this behaviour from me and that I will be unable to help them because I have never been able to stop pulling. If I consider only myself, then I want to stop pulling my hair out to improve the quality of my life, and to increase my chances of living a long life, too. I feel that I need to beat hair pulling in order to put all this negativity behind me, and that I need to stop pulling my hair so that I can begin to enjoy life and give my children the upbringing that I want them to have.

14. Do you want to pull other people's hair out?

No! This is a funny question. I can say that in general terms I have no interest in other people's hair, or at least no more interest than the average person. I'm not even sure I have an objective, conscious interest in my own hair. It is the sensation of moving my hair that I get from my hands and from my skin that I enjoy. That being said, strangely enough, now that I have children there are occasions when I have noticed a hair standing up and I have been half-tempted to pull it out. Maybe it is because in some way my children feel like extensions of myself, I'm not sure. I have never had an impulse to pull anyone else's hair out other than this.

15. How would you feel if a friend told you they pulled their hair out, too?

I would be entirely compassionate. I also think that initially I might be quite excited at the news. Until very recently I had never talked to another person who has the same relationship with their hair the way I do and I would feel excited to talk and share experiences. I would want to ask some big questions like: do you ever think you are insane? What is your self-esteem like? Are you scared of what other people might think about you for pulling your hair? I think I could be a good resource for a friend with this problem. I think I am naturally a compassionate person who is interested in other people's motivations and in helping them.

16. What have you tried doing to stop it?

I have tried nearly everything. I have tried wearing gloves, wearing a hat, putting gel and other hair products in my hair. I have tried pulling an elastic band at my wrist every time I catch myself either pulling a hair out or having an urge to do so. I have tried sitting on my hands, keeping my left hand busy (it is almost always my left-hand that is the culprit). The best thing that works for me is shaving my hair so short that I cannot readily pull hairs out. I came upon this technique about twenty years ago and I have maintained a short hair-cut ever since. It's okay because I am male; most female hair pullers are reluctant to crop their hair short and I feel so very sorry for them.

17. What advice would you give to other hair pullers?

Always believe in yourself. You are no more crazy than the next person. You have a very unfortunate habit that marks you out as an individual, but you are no crazier than somebody who cannot stop biting their nails, or who nervously bites their lip. You just have a nervous habit and you need to accept that you have this problem. Everybody has problems of one sort or another so it is okay. You are okay. The shame and sadness that you feel can ruin your life if you let them. You have to keep fighting to stay afloat, and never give in to the idea that there is nothing you can do to help yourself. Do not let trichotillomania ruin you for it is only one small aspect of the whole person you are.

18. What have you learned from trichotillomania?

I have mainly learned that I am not fully in charge of my own behaviour. This was a hard lesson to learn because it runs counter to everything that we believe about ourselves as intelligent, reflexive human adults. I can no more stop myself from pulling hair than I can stop myself from breathing, and it is not the conscious me who tells my body to breath. It is not the conscious me who pulls out my hair.

I have learned the hard way that I am an imperfect and fallible human being. I have learned to let go of my tendency for perfectionism. I have learned that when I pull my hair out I am not 'in the room', I am somewhere else in my mind, reliving the past, projecting into the future or somehow abstracted. I have learned the importance of inhabiting the present, and practising mindfulness has helped me get here.

19. Does an online community help?

Yes and no. It was a powerful safety net for me when I found that there are web-based communities for hair pullers, and that these websites hosted lots of personal stories from other people who were suffering. I have learned so much about the disorder from the internet and from the people who organise online communities. I am eternally indebted to them. I have read personal accounts of trichotillomania that have moved me to tears. These records of everyday human suffering helped me to learn that I was not alone, that if I were a freak then there are plenty of other freaks just like me locked in to their own private and shameful hells.

101

Where online communities sometimes might not help, in my opinion, is when trichotillomania becomes an important bond between people, and an important way for people to feel special. As an example, one of the first things I read in an online forum was that people who pull their hair tend to be highly intelligent. This piece of information made me feel good because I wanted to identify with it. It begins to make you want to have trichotillomania in your life because although it can be viewed as a curse it marks you out from the crowd in a good way. I don't buy into these ideas now. I have no reason to believe that this illness affects only clever people; it smells like bullshit to me, the kind of bullshit that rewards you for pulling out your hair and won't ever let you beat it.

20. What do you think your future holds?

Good things, I hope! Once I get this book off my desk I plan to write a novel with any spare time I can find. I will strive to keep perfectionism at bay and just hammer it out on the keyboard. I have dreamed of writing a novel for such a long time and now I feel that I will turn that dream into reality.

We are expecting a third baby at the moment. I hope that my wife and baby come out of it healthy and happy. I look forward to spending the next ten to fifteen years raising our children with my wife.

There is nothing more important to me than this. While I hold the fear that my children may inherit trichotillomania from me I also have good grounds to hope that they won't. The family environment they live in is different from the one that I grew up in. Okay, they will get half of their genes from me, but hopefully the good ones only! I have faith that they will grow up without this disorder but then again even if the worst happens and one of them does begin pulling out their hair then I will be in the best place to help them with it. My reaction would not be the same as my parents' reactions.

Philip Larkin has a poem about the way in which parents influence their children for the worse. He describes a deeply grim view about successive generations transmitting increasingly negative traits from one to the next. When I was sixteen I shared his view. Today I don't. With love and compassion as guiding forces, I think each generation can become incrementally better than the last. So I walk forward in hope.